Sukkot

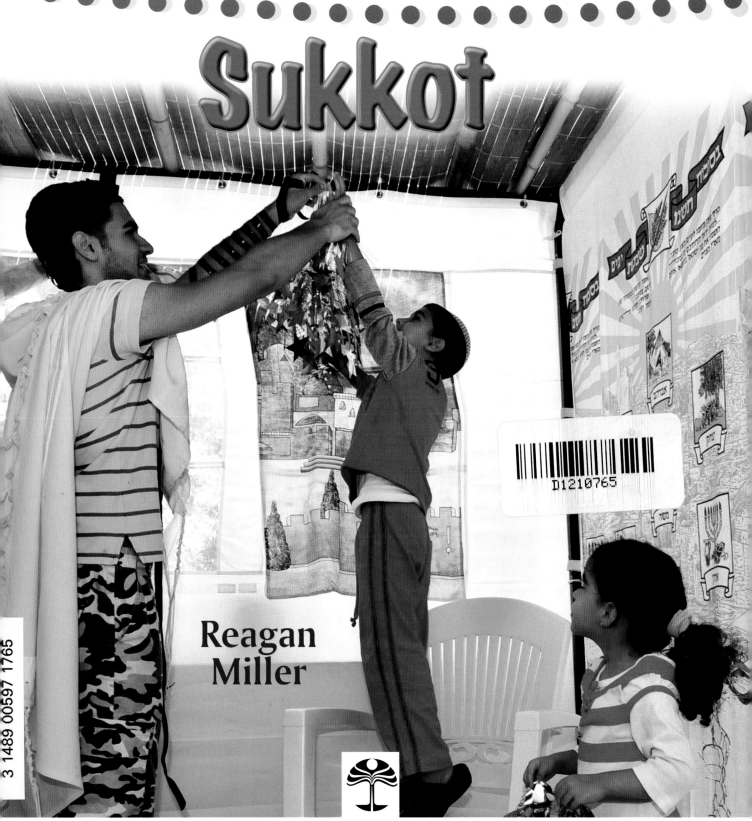

Reagan
Miller

Crabtree Publishing Company
www.crabtreebooks.com

Crabtree Publishing Company
www.crabtreebooks.com

Author: Reagan Miller
Coordinating editor: Chester Fisher
Series and project editor: Susan LaBella
Editor: Adrianna Morganelli
Proofreader: Molly Aloian
Editorial director: Kathy Middleton
Production coordinator: Katherine Berti
Prepress technician: Katherine Berti
Project manager: Kumar Kunal (Q2AMEDIA)
Art direction: Rahul Dhiman (Q2AMEDIA)
Cover design: Shruti Aggarwal (Q2AMEDIA)
Design: Cheena Yadav (Q2AMEDIA)
Photo research: Ekta Sharma (Q2AMEDIA)

Photographs:
AFP: Menahem Kahana: p. 16
Alamy: Israel images: p. 9, 20
AP Photo: Kevin Frayer: p. 11
BigStockPhoto: David Davis: p. 25
Corbis: Andy Aitchison: p. 13; Bettmann: p. 23
Dreamstime: Frenk and Danielle Kaufmann: p. 30; Rainer Schmittchen: p. 7
Fotolia: Sonya Etchison: p. 5; Graham Photography: p. 6; Noam: p. 18
Getty Images: Fred Mayer/Contributor: p. 15, 22; David Silverman/
    Staff: p. 12
Istockphoto: Noam Armonn: p. 19; Lisa Turay: p. 31
Photolibrary: North Wind Pictures: p. 10; Dan Porges: cover (background),
    p. 14, 27; Con Tanasiuk: p. 24
Photoshot: Chameleons Eye: p. 1
Reuters: Gil Cohen Magen: p. 26; Abed Omar Qusini: p. 17
Shutterstock: cover (foreground), folio image; MoonBloom: p. 21; Pjasha: p. 8
World Religions: Christine Osborne Pictures: p. 28, 29

Library and Archives Canada Cataloguing in Publication

Miller, Reagan
     Sukkot / Reagan Miller.

(Celebrations in my world)
Includes index.
ISBN 978-0-7787-4766-6 (bound).--ISBN 978-0-7787-4784-0 (pbk.)

     1. Sukkot--Juvenile literature. I. Title.
II. Series: Celebrations in my world

BM695.S8M54 2009   j296.4'33   C2009-905272-5

Library of Congress Cataloging-in-Publication Data

Miller, Reagan.
 Sukkot / Reagan Miller.
     p. cm. -- (Celebrations in my world)
 Includes index.
 ISBN 978-0-7787-4784-0 (pbk. : alk. paper) -- ISBN 978-0-7787-4766-6
(reinforced library binding : alk. paper)
 1. Sukkot--Juvenile literature. I. Title. II. Series.

 BM695.S8M55 2010
 296.4'33--dc22

                                        2009035005

Crabtree Publishing Company

www.crabtreebooks.com   1-800-387-7650   Printed in China/122009/CT20090915

Published in Canada
Crabtree Publishing
616 Welland Ave.
St. Catharines, ON
L2M 5V6

Published in the United States
Crabtree Publishing
350 Fifth Ave.
59th floor
New York, NY 10118

Published in the United Kingdom
Crabtree Publishing
Maritime House
Basin Road North, Hove
BN41 1WR

Published in Australia
Crabtree Publishing
386 Mt. Alexander Rd.
Ascot Vale (Melbourne)
VIC 3032

Contents

What is Sukkot?

Sukkot is one of three main holidays celebrated by people of the Jewish religion. Sukkot is celebrated in September or October. The dates of the holiday change from year to year but it always takes place during autumn.

Jewish people use a Jewish calendar. Sukkot is celebrated on the 15th day of the seventh month.

September 2010
...lul 5766 - 8 Tishrei 5767

		Wed	Thu	Fri	Sat
		1 8 Elul	2 9 Elul Ki Tetze	3 10 Elul	4 11 Elul	5 12 Elul
6 13 Elul	7 14 Elul	8 15 Elul	9 16 Elul Ki Tavo	10 17 Elul	11 18 Elul	12 19 Elul
13 20 Elul	14 21 Elul	15 22 Elul	16 23 Elul S'lichot (evening) Nitzavim/Vayeledh	17 24 Elul	18 25 Elul	19 26 Elul
20 27 Elul	21 28 Elul	22 29 Elul Erev R H	23	24	25 Tishrei	26 4 Tishrei
27 5 Tishre						

DID YOU KNOW?

Jewish people believe sunset signals the start of a new day. Sukkot and many other Jewish holidays begin at sunset for this reason.

Sukkot is celebrated for seven days and seven nights. It is one of the most cheerful Jewish holidays. It is a time when Jewish people remember their history, celebrate God's love, and are thankful for all they have.

Sukkot takes place in autumn, or fall. In many places, the leaves change color and fall from the trees.

What is Judaism?

The Jewish religion is called Judaism. Judaism is one of the oldest religions. It began nearly 4,000 years ago. Judaism is practiced by millions of people around the world. Judaism teaches that there is one God who is the creator of all things.

People who practice Judaism study the holy book called the Torah.

Judaism also teaches Jewish people to treat others with kindness and to help people in need. Helping others is an important part of celebrating Sukkot.

- A **synagogue** is a building where Jewish people go to pray.

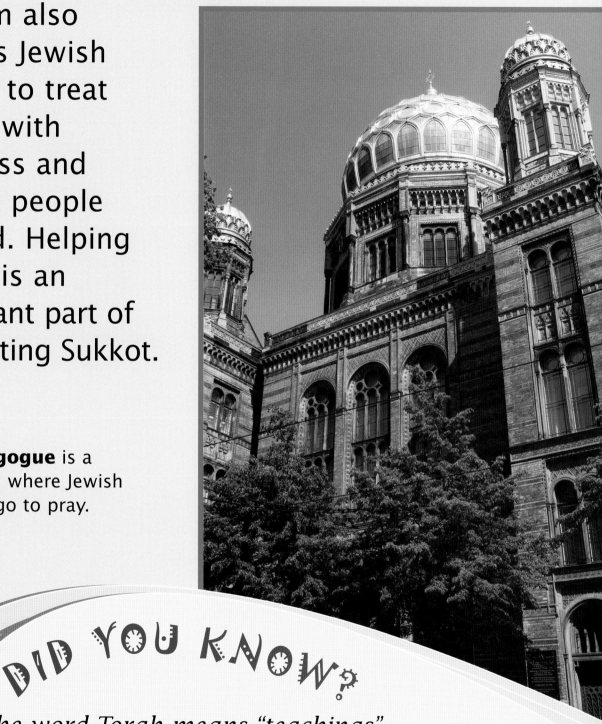

DID YOU KNOW?

The word Torah means "teachings" in the Hebrew language. The Torah teaches Jewish people how God wants them to live their lives.

The History of Sukkot

Sukkot celebrates Jewish history. Long ago, Jewish people lived as **slaves** in Egypt. God told Moses to lead the Jewish people out of Egypt and guide them to Israel. They spent 40 years walking through the desert before reaching Israel.

• The Jewish people walked through the Sinai desert to reach Israel.

Mediterranean Sea

Israel

Egypt

Sinai Desert

Red Sea

Middle East

This kind of booth is called a sukkah.

It was a difficult journey but God cared for the Jewish people. God made sure they had food, water, and shelter. During Sukkot, Jewish people remember how God cared for their **ancestors** during their journey to Israel.

DID YOU KNOW?

During their journey, God told the Jewish people to build booths for shelter. These booths were called sukkot. One booth is called a sukkah. The booths protected the Jewish people day and night.

9

Remembering the Harvest

During Sukkot, Jewish people also celebrate their ancestors' way of life. Many Jewish people became farmers once they reached Israel. The farmers **harvested** their **crops** in autumn. The crops had to be picked quickly so they did not spoil, or rot.

- Long ago, farmers did all of the work by hand. They did not have machines to help them like we do today.

During the harvest, a farmer would build a sukkah in his field. He slept in the sukkah so he could begin picking crops in the early morning without having to travel to the field from home. After the harvest, people praised God for providing them with the harvested food.

Children take part in a Sukkot pilgrimage, or trip, to thank God for the harvest.

DID YOU KNOW?

There are holidays to celebrate the autumn harvest in many places around the world. For example, in North America, many people celebrate a holiday called Thanksgiving.

Celebrate with a Sukkah

The sukkah is an important **symbol** of Sukkot. In the days leading up to Sukkot, many Jewish families are busy building their sukkah. Some build a sukkah in their backyards or on **balconies**.

In the Torah, God tells the Jewish people they must "dwell" in a sukkah for seven days.

DID YOU KNOW?

Sukkot is the Hebrew word for "booths." The holiday, Sukkot, is sometimes called the Festival of the Booths.

Other people work together to build a sukkah at their synagogue. During Sukkot, Jewish families eat, pray, and visit with friends and family in a sukkah. They are to think of their sukkah as home. Some people even sleep in a sukkah!

This boy is sleeping in his family's colorful sukkah.

Building a Sukkah

There are rules for building a sukkah. A sukkah must have at least two complete walls and the start of a third wall. The walls must be strong enough to stay standing when it is windy. A sukkah's roof must be made from plant parts that once grew from the ground, such as corn stalks or tree branches.

A sukkah can be small for just one person or large enough for hundreds of people.

A sukkah's roof is called the S'chach.

The roof must provide shelter to protect people from the sun. It must also have openings large enough for people to see the moon and stars at night.

DID YOU KNOW?

Sukkot is a time for people to feel close to nature. Spending time in a sukkah helps people connect with nature. Inside a sukkah, people can feel the sun, rain, and wind.

A Snazzy Sukkah!

Once the sukkah is built, it is time to decorate it! The sukkah is meant to be a cheerful place. Children often enjoy making decorations for the sukkah.

Children draw colorful pictures and banners or make mobiles to hang in their sukkah.

DID YOU KNOW?

Many people decorate their sukkah with fruits and vegetables from the autumn harvest. These decorations remind people to be thankful to God for helping the crops grow.

Children can show respect for Earth by making decorations using **recycled** materials. For example, children can use recycled paper to make paper chains to hang inside a sukkah. Children can decorate paper tissue rolls to make napkin rings to use during meals inside the sukkah.

Some people decorate using plastic fruits and vegetables so food is not wasted.

The Celebration Begins

The sukkah should be ready for the start of Sukkot. The celebration begins at sunset, and the first holiday meal starts soon after. Families eat meals together in their sukkah. On the first night of Sukkot, people welcome the celebration by saying a **blessing** and then lighting holiday candles.

A woman usually lights the Sukkot holiday candles.

18

A man says the Kiddush before the meal.

People say Kiddush, or a special holiday prayer, before the meal begins. They thank God for the blessing of the holiday and all that God has provided.

DID YOU KNOW?

The first two days of Sukkot are days of rest. People are not to do any work. The only work that is allowed is preparing meals.

A Scrumptious Sukkot!

Sukkot is a celebration of the autumn harvest. Many delicious meals prepared during this holiday are made from fresh fall fruits and vegetables.

This family is enjoying a delicious meal inside their sukkah.

Foods such as corn, pumpkins, pomegranates, apples, cranberries, and grapes are popular at this time of year. Soups and stews are often served during this holiday because they help keep people warm while eating outdoors in the sukkah.

People give thanks to God for a plentiful harvest.

DID YOU KNOW?

You can build a delicious sukkah! Use graham crackers and icing to make the walls. Use pretzels or cereal to make the roof. Decorate your sukkah with bits of fruit.

21

Sharing with Others

Sukkot is a time to be generous and to share. People invite family, friends, and neighbors to their sukkah to enjoy a meal together. People who are not Jewish are also welcome in the sukkah.

Family and friends share with one another at a Sukkot meal.

In some communities, families plan "Sukkah Hops." Each family makes a treat for others to enjoy. Families then walk from sukkah to sukkah enjoying the treats and visiting with friends.

- The seven holy guests are known as the "Seven Shepherds of Israel." Moses is one of the holy guests.

DID YOU KNOW?

On each night of Sukkot, Jewish people pray and invite a holy guest to their sukkah. The guests are Abraham, Moses, and other ancestors from the Torah.

Helping Others

During Sukkot, Jewish people give thanks to God for providing shelter and food. It is also a time to think about people who are in need. Some people collect food to give to food banks.

Sukkot is a time to give to others in need. This boy is giving food to people in need at a shelter.

Others help out at homeless shelters during the holiday. At some synagogues, people raise money to give to **charities** that work to help end hunger around the world.

● Some people make lists of the things they are thankful for. People can share these things with family and friends.

DID YOU KNOW?

Children can help people in need by collecting canned food to give to food banks. Children can also give their old clothing and toys to charities that can give them to children in need.

25

The Four Species

One of the most important symbols of Sukkot is called the four species. The four species are four different kinds of plants that grow in Israel. They include three types of branches and one kind of fruit.

Some people spend days looking for the most beautiful examples of each of the four species.

The four plants are myrtle, willow, palm shoot, and citron. During Sukkot, people use the four species for a special blessing. These four plants grow naturally in Israel.

Outside of Israel, they are shipped and sold in markets in the weeks before Sukkot.

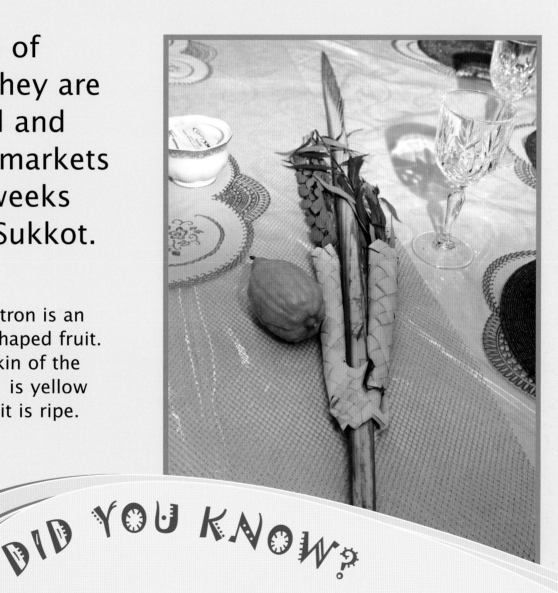

- The citron is an oval-shaped fruit. The skin of the citron is yellow when it is ripe.

DID YOU KNOW?

The myrtle, willow, and palm are tied together to form a lulav. *The citron, called an* etrog, *is kept separate from the* lulav.

Waves of Blessings

The four species are used in a special blessing every day during Sukkot except for on the **Sabbath**. The *lulav* is held in one hand and the *etrog* is held in the other.

A special blessing is said while waving the four species in all six directions—north, south, east, west, up, and down.

- A young boy holds the four plants as he says the special blessing.

This is done to celebrate the Jewish belief that God is everywhere. On the seventh day of Sukkot, people gather at a synagogue and perform a final blessing using the four species.

- The special blessing is done inside a sukkah or in a synagogue.

DID YOU KNOW?

Sukkot is celebrated before the rainy season begins in Israel. At the end of Sukkot, people pray to God for enough rain for plants to grow in the spring.

A Sukkot Snack

Sukkot is a wonderful time to enjoy the fruits, vegetables, and grains from the autumn harvest. Different kinds of foods are grown in different parts of the world.

Find out what kinds of foods are grown in your community. Let an adult help you use these foods to make a Sukkot snack, such as fruit salad.

● You can share your snack with family and friends.

Share your healthy treats with family and friends in your sukkah. Treats such as roasted pumpkin seeds and fruit salad are nutritious and delicious!

Harvest Fruit Salad: Choose fresh fruits grown in your area. Ask an adult to help you wash them and cut them into small pieces.

DID YOU KNOW?

Sukkot is a good time to visit a farm or orchard. You will learn which fruits and vegetables grow there. Sometimes, you can help pick your own fruits or vegetables to take home.

31

Glossary

ancestor One from whom a person or group of people is descended

balconies Platforms built at the side of buildings

blessing Asking for care and protection for something

charities Organizations that help people in need

crop A plant that can be grown and harvested

harvest The gathering of a crop; also the season when crops are gathered

recycled Things used more than once rather than being thrown away

Sabbath A Jewish holy day of rest and worship. It takes place each week from sunset on Friday to sunset on Saturday

slaves People who are owned by other people and forced to do hard work

symbol Something that stands for something else

synagogue A building where Jewish people worship

Index